THE WRONG SIDE OF THE CURTAIN

OTHER BOOKS BY MARC CREAMORE

TEA LEAVES AND DENIM

BLEAKER STREET AND OTHER OBSERVATIONS

CORRIDORS

CORRIDORS is also available in CD format (featuring the author's narration of a selection of poems from the book CORRIDORS, recited against ambient backgrounds of nature and music).

All titles available by contacting:

Frog Hollow Books
1164 Forge Walk
Vancouver, B.C.
V6H 3P9
Phone: (604) 739 3633
Fax: (604) 739 0177
website: www.froghollowbooks.com
email: froghollowbooks@shaw.ca

THE WRONG SIDE OF THE CURTAIN

MARC CREAMORE

FROG HOLLOWBOOKS
VANCOUVER, B.C.

First Edition.

Cover design, layout and photographs by Donna Harasemchuk.

Cover and inside pages printed on recycled stock.

Library and Archives Canada Cataloguing in Publication

Creamore, Marc, 1949-
The wrong side of the curtain / Marc Creamore. -- 1st ed.

Poems.
ISBN 0-9681997-6-3

I. Title.

PS8555.R412W76 2004 C811'.54 C2004-904553-9

Orders, comments, and inquiries:

Frog Hollow Books
1164 Forge Walk
Vancouver, B.C.
V6H 3P9
Phone: (604) 739 3633
Fax: (604) 739 0177
email: froghollowbooks@shaw.ca
website: www.froghollowbooks.com

PRINTED AND BOUND IN CANADA

For Donna

"Why can't we all just walk away?"

— David Tibet

TABLE OF CONTENTS

PREFACE

THE WRONG SIDE OF THE CURTAIN — screams of planetary assault and hermetic whispers sent out across these pages culled from an aching pen since the first day of the new millennium. Starts off with recognition of veil of illusion and all its silly-fied causes — revisits horrifying holocaust of Middle East crisis — crashes into Self, seeking answers regarding my own mortality and hidden secrets of other dimensions — moans for birds and garden of Earth, ponders poetry game and its internal anguish — then laments the cavalcade of antiquity as it passes before the historical screen of mankind. I question my seemingly over abundant negativity — then stop short — watch T.V. newscasts more threatening than Bay Of Pigs of my childhood and come to realize why these dark, cloudy poems came to be conceived.

Second part bids adieu to Black Angel of Destruction and attempts to address possibilities of previous incarnations and Buddha thought alive, but asleep inside the mind — offers thankyous to Rimbaud, Ginsberg and other prophets of wide awake word — then touches the spinning wheel of existence and the undiscovered frontier of non-artificial wisdom.

The last section of the book draws inspiration from the quietude of pastoral settings — breathes inside moonlit visitations, the laughter of koto and goldfinch — nostalgically looks back at childhood and memories of comradery when there was always enough Zen in the pocket — then floats through a dreamscape of undisturbed meditation and closes with a prayer that we will one day touch one another with the language of universal heart.

July 9th, 2004

THE AGE OLD APOCALYPTIC BLUES

PLEASE DON'T TAKE THIS POEM TOO SERIOUSLY

Please don't take this poem too seriously
because it's only a torn blind on a broken window pane,
it's only my ripped apart tongue
bleeding on an invisible page,
only a child unwilling to sleep
while her father tries to get down a line or two,
only a dog snoring
inside his karmic continuance,
only a broken heater
within the walls of an igloo,
only the torn sandal of Christ
on that final day,
only a chewed up ball
disguised as a star,
only a suitcase
full of unrealized dreams,
only a bare lightbulb
smothered by one million moths,
only a backgammon game
devoid of players,
only a planet
covered in the grime of mortal existence,
where an old poet
sits grumbling at his broken down desk,
taking himself

too

seriously.

BIRTHDAY POEM

52 years old and still I am alive,
still breathing, still hypnotized by the echo of my own
voice, calling out into the music box
of the universe.

All these years of thought,
reflecting off the mirror inside my aching skull,
tiny contemplations, yet to be fertilized in the soil
of the mind.

When young,
I roamed the shoreline of imagination, turned over
shells in the sand, sought minuscule life forms
and wept like a child into the oncoming
wave of adulthood.

Adulthood with its secret paper of pain,
adulthood where the bigger questions made their
presence felt, sticking neurotic fingers into my ribs,
causing the heart to tremble before the inevitable
mask of mortality.

Women, wine and song,
naive belief systems, rushing from one cave to another,
books of rapture held in the earthquake
of my hands.

I spent days and nights
locked up in a room, blue lightbulb and marijuana,
incense and music, the lyrical oratory of folk
singers. Were they the minstrels of a new dawn,
or only dissatisfied poets, trying to escape the nightmare
they found themselves in?

I staggered through doorways,
repented with false icons and broken angels,
but redemption was as far away as a drunken vision

of Christ . . . when morning yawned I was still bleeding
behind hung over eyes.

I tasted the Buddha fish,
licked its perfect saffron scales, yet found myself
swimming through an ocean
of samsaric coral.

No avalanche from the mountain
of wisdom, no glacial stream in which to bathe
my parched soul . . . just fragile seraphim that
I thought were true, only to discover that they too
had relinquished their birthright, wings crippled,
unable to transcend the mythological border
of flesh and bones.

Birth, death, silence and cacophony . . .
yin-yang juxtaposition, battling like demented
lemmings inside the confused chambers
of the mind.

Oh why must it be so difficult
to achieve clarification of existential purpose?
Why do stumbling moths still ignore the light buried
behind my eyes?

Yes, flesh and bones,
beginning to feel the ancient shadow approaching . . .

52 years
and still so long to go on the pilgrimage
I have chosen.

THE WRONG SIDE OF THE CURTAIN

We're standing like forlorn ghosts,
watching a dead parade pass by with it's legacy
of dark secrets,
While one million harmonicas wail on the wrong side
of the curtain.

Oh the wrong side of the curtain,
the veil of truth inverted, turned inside out,
Where druids chant beside the burning ash can
of an international ghetto
Where we dress our eyes in a fable of brutality
Where the genetic mystery keeps slamming the door
shut because it's imprint was corrupted from
the very beginning of time
Where industrial clowns cavort with siliconed sirens,
Make derelict love in the basements of the towers
on Wall Street
While a few blocks away an Afro-American saint puts
his mouth to a tenor saxophone
and weeps.

Oh the wrong side of the curtain
where a deranged monk stands in an empty
courtyard
And embraces texts of separation with his bleeding
hands
Where a poet whispers from a flaming pyre of bones
Where an old man sits on a forgotten ledge
and contemplates an ancient prophecy gone bad
Where a singular eye gazes down to penetrate
the inner heart of humanity,
And finds it vacant, even after all these years,
all these simple clues,
All these aches and trembling reverberations
that have made little or no difference
Because difference is frowned upon by the diviners
of economic thrust.

Oh the wrong side of the curtain
where we become the creases in the rotting garment
of a dead mystic
Where we fall down in the crow black night
and try to cleanse ourselves with a bar of soap
in a muddy river
Where we pray in pews like broken clarinets
Where locusts keep hungrily dancing across
the prairies,
Even though the band laid down it's instruments
a couple of Centuries ago
When Europe disabled the buffalo and the dove
flapped her white wings and flew to a cave
of silence
That was once the echo chamber of the initial utterance
from the mouth of Creation.

Oh the wrong side of the curtain
where we resurrect a manifesto of inconceivable
graffiti
Where we witness naked fear and become rag dolls
in the rain
Where a hobo weeps without a boxcar
Where the Madonna tucks her white unkissed breast
into a rough hewn garment,
Feels her face wrinkle and crack beneath the paint
of a surreal canvas
And goes stumbling down through the annuls of time
in search of an immaculate stable.

Oh the wrong side of the curtain
where the engine travels on a crooked track
Where we finally arrive at the station and discover
that the train left 10 minutes ago
Where Edison's ghost laughs all the way
to Hollywood
Where the dead man climbs out of his catacomb,
dusts the cobwebs from his eyes,
Puts on his historically moth eaten robe
and reenters the coliseum
Which is still a nightmare of hopeless aggression
even after a couple of millenniums of sleep.

Oh the wrong side of the curtain
    where the forest is seduced by the sickness
    of a chemical firefly
Where we all bear the same maggot infested burden
Where the angels left without telling us why
Where the old jeweler closes his blinds,
    turns off the light
And staggers home to his wife and children who play
    video games
Until it's time to collapse into a bed devoid of dreams
    or possibilities of imagination.

Oh the wrong side of the curtain
    where the literary waterfall of Japan evaporates
    beneath a polluted moon
Where the beer soaked bar stool of separation is never
    empty
Where the void contains one billion spirits
    who stagger across the ever moving sand
Where Robert Johnson trades his guitar for a shovel,
    sits down at the crossroads of Main
    and Armageddon
And discusses the burial grounds still to come
    with St. John of the Cross.

Oh the wrong side of the curtain
    where the ashes and stench of spiritual decay
    blacken the nostrils of beauty
Where even holy ground can sometimes blister the feet
Where our bones yellow beneath the moist Earth
    and its' centipedes and blossoms
Where Walt Whitman gazes across the fields
    of what used to be America,
Shakes a defiant fist and realizing that
    the leviathan that crawls before him is numb
    to his once listened to words,
Drifts back to the poets' round table and sips
    from a mystical grail with William Blake.

Oh the wrong side of the curtain
    where across the street the last folk singer
    hangs himself with a guitar string

Where a New Age philosopher picks up the remains
of a distant prayer and casts it aside like an empty
cigarette case
Where the laughter of a cicada is captured in
the 3rd movement of a dead symphony
Where the implementation of the plans for the next
millennium is laid out upon a desk
Where the reality of starvation and poverty is ignored
and the Third World is a gnat that creates
an itch somewhere in the wrinkled brow
of the United Nations
Even though the Third World has spoken forcefully
in an explosion of absolute fury and desperation,
Towers collapsing like dominoes upon the carpet
of democracy.

Oh the wrong side of the curtain
where sparrows pray that the sun won't fall
from the sky
Where bardic fathers moan on the banks of swollen
rivers
Where we are sodomized by a shadowy hallucination
of relentless lust
Where a sunflower wilts outside a rusting iron gate,
collects the dust and deathly matter of diesel fueled
machinery
And tries to reflect an image of abundance,
all the while coughing and sputtering like
a displaced salmon.

Oh the wrong side of the curtain
where skyscrapers stand like sentinels
And watch over cities that only perpetuate a continuum
of death, death, death
Where tired raindrops pound upon broken window
panes and snowflakes are scarred by battery acid
Where the hunchback strains every muscle
in an attempt to keep the planet's orbit on course
Where we enter the ballroom wearing boots
of debauchery
Where we tear at a parasite that will never leave
the flesh

Where havoc is created beneath a tree of candles
Where white crosses weather like rotten teeth
in the mouth of humanity
Where the generals are busy conspiring a new
nightmare
Where the song being heard on the airwaves
is the age old apocalyptic blues
Where we can no longer walk out into the light
of breathing ivy
Where green expanses fail to overgrow archaic
battlefields
Where the laurels of the past are nothing but
a lonely tomb
And where I sit here in some dark compartment
of my mind
Scribbling a black litany out into the Universe
in the hopes that some alien scientist,
some until now unseen messiah
or some radiant cosmic child
Will reach beyond this unacceptable malaise
and with a translucent hand

RIP THIS

ILLUSIONARY CURTAIN

ASUNDER.

THE MEN OF THIS WORLD

Oh my lover,
what good are these words
if I cannot create a place of beauty
where we can be free of this tragedy
called the world?

Men barter their children,
their wives and their parents
for a little piece of gluttony's action.

Lover,
the collective soul is diminishing
and the loins at the edge of the once
living womb are drying up.

I cannot in my discouraged state
even begin to make a bed of roses
lit by candlelight.

Outside the window I can hear
the tubercular cough of a chickadee,
the river's desperate moan,
the sorrowful sigh of the moon
as she limps across the heavens.

Is this to be our final instalment,
a prophet's nightmare come true,
where we can't even find a garden
to birth our children in?

History marches with a leper's feet,
blood caked toes staining the very ground
we try to make love upon.

Mankind declares the death of God,
without comprehending what the psychological
concept of God was meant to be.

And so as I hold you
in the stillness of this night,
here inside this window,
inside this bed of no roses
or candlelight,

Here where I can see divinity
staring at me from your eyes,

I weep . . .

because the men of this world
still wander down halls of gluttony

and because if God isn't dead

then he is at least exhaling
his final

breath.

THE GARDEN IS SICK

The garden is sick, the garden is ailing,
spinning like a wounded albatross
    through the vast domain
        of space,
      weeping, moaning . . .
        but her cries,

                they go unheeded.

We forget to caress her soft green vulva,
instead, we ignore her aching urgency to pro-create,
    dismiss her fertile dance,
      blemish her once verdant breasts
        with uncaring fingers.
Her sap driven blood coagulates,
    can't even nourish the tiniest of life forms . . .
Amphibians born with a multitude of limbs,
    birds hatched without eyes
      and trees rotting in a soil made too weak
        to feed elongated roots.

WHAT HAVE WE DONE . . .
                OH WHAT HAVE WE DONE?

We have almost murdered the Earth,
    not realizing that our hands

    hold the weapon.

OH THAT WE SHOULD BREAK BREAD WITH GNOMES OF DARKNESS

As this century turns, I sit in the dark,
light incense and realize that nothing
ever really changes.

Middle East crisis, Jerusalem holy war,
going back thousands of years,
comes forward to the present with suicide bombs
and a hatred conceived in the womb of history.

No, nothing ever really changes,
as this sadness hymn is continuously written
on newsprint of political aggression,
while babies shake rattles and giggle
from cradles of poverty.

Across the planet millions
march for peace . . . the very young, old hippies,
the doctors, the lawyers, the elderly. . .
from Moscow to Montreal,
from Bangkok to Naples . . .
while the American hawk vows
to slaughter his prey.

Satanic moans emanate from a sky inflamed,
while four horsemen gallop without direction
and so called holy books are thrown
from the withered hands of prophets into a caldron
resplendent with past nightmares and future
holocausts.

Oh must we be merely the fruit
that Christ turned into wine,
are we only to be remembered as a colony of lepers,
unable to escape the hurling of stones,
spiritually dis-eased and in need
of a ladder?

Yes, nothing ever really changes
because we live in a time where we do not feel
the nails being driven into our hands,
we live in a time where an Iraqi child weeps
beside a mosque . . . while some diplomat
on the other side of the world plots a military strategy,
that with one swipe of the pen,
could murder millions without regret.

So many years of living in a thimble,
questioning the depth of the Universe,
waiting for the explosion of clocks,
waiting for the conundrum of the final deep sleep
to be solved.

We wander beneath ancient clouds,
consider not the sad spaces of silence that grow
between the notes of mankind's insipid,
historical symphony.

The decay of the soul has reached
epidemic proportions . . .
while the body is emancipated with diet,
with AIDS, with bulimia . . .
and the mind schizophrenic
and molested in dark rooms where the language
of biological pleasure curses toddlers and women
without restriction.

Gluttony and greed extinguish
the small light of the world,
the small light that desperately clings
to the tattered and torn garment of a mythological god,
while shadows of deceit lengthen.

Oh I try to dream past the shards
of broken, stained glass,
past the cries of parentless children . . .
but my dream is haunted by a vision of unmerciful
omnipotence,
by the foolish fairy tale spinner
who dances across the horizon

with caustic feet.

We pray before a rusty door that never opens,
our sacred books are written in blood
and the planet is decorated
with a multitude of flags of divisive
colour.

Civilizations they pass,
are glorified in text books, in lecture halls
and art galleries,
while the only difference
between the caveman and today's world leaders is a
belligerent briefcase.

And while we rest in stupefied splendor,
the Universe waits for the day when the warring factions
gather upon the plains of heaven to commence
the final battle.

No, nothing ever really changes
and as I suffer, you too suffer . . .
we all suffer in our own individualized suffering.
We fling ourselves toward the arms
of a crucifixion tree,
oblivious to the beauty we carry
within us.

We are falling, falling and lost,
unable to grasp the wings of the mysterious bird
who flies beyond this landscape littered with shrapnel
and artificial happiness.

AH, THAT WE SHOULD BE SO BLIND
IN A WORLD WHERE TREES REACH
FOR THE STARS!
THAT WE SHOULD BE SO OLD
AND CRANKY WITHOUT MAGIC
IN THE HEART!
THAT WE SHOULD BREAK BREAD
WITH GNOMES OF DARKNESS,

FORGETFUL THAT OUR CHILDREN
STILL FIND JOY IN THE DELICACY
OF A BUTTERFLY'S WING!

No, nothing ever really changes,
but as the final chapter is recited like a poem
in a mortuary,
I utter a prayer
and watch as the hierarchy of the damned
and all their deadening tablets of pain
melt in my tear-stained
hands.

THE FOOL SITS ON A HILL

Oh the fool sits on a hill,
wrapped in saffron, prayer beads broken,
stone cold in meditation,
mumbling a monotone
mantra . . .

Oh where be the grace,
the calm before the fall,
before the poem became dead prose,
before the sun shone down on this now
empty world,
where the words of the wise
seem to be ignored?

THE ONE MILLION BUDDHAS

I keep banging my fist against the veil,
trying to push through the translucent skin,
where I can simply be a daffodil in a vase
on a table
inside an invisible monastery
where the one million Buddhas write sutras
for future generations.

From the beginning of time
we have somehow failed to come to terms
with the gestation of the non-biological embryo
growing within the womb
of the spirit.

Oh the odd sage,
the odd soothsayer has recognized its importance,
understood the evolutionary principle
that the wise have touched
throughout history.

But too few have unmasked its mystery,
too few have escaped the confines of the body
and flew like joyful hummingbirds
toward a nectar of knowing.

A dark aura of complacency
still enshrouds the globe,
the pain of living still reveals
wounds unhealed,
still weeps, still trembles,
encrusted with a deep sorrow
that has not been addressed,
alleviated with a soothing balm
of insight.

The one million Buddhas sit between
time and space
and chant words of compassion

out into the cosmos.

MISCONSTRUED IN BLUE

It's almost November
and I am Bunny Berrigan's horn in "I Can't Get Started".

Lassitude lingers,
broken fingernails scratch on some blackboard
in the back of my mind.

And there's paper everywhere,
all subterranean and without substance,
half-baked metaphors made by the bastardized
split in my tongue.

Even the clouds suffer today,
while the constant rising and falling of my chest cavity
makes me aware that I am still here.

Here scribbling in the madness
of non-communication.
Here with my pen
like a dull razor upon the beard of the page,
trying to make some sense of drunken
politicians and poets who starve inside beds
of human ice.

I see the image of my face
staring at me from the nearest mud puddle.
A decaying leaf smiles and says:
"Impermanence is the lifeblood of the heavens . . .
it makes us minions or sages.
It all depends on the interpretation".

I look at the beauty of my sleeping child
and I am unnerved by the ghost of my own passing.
I scream that I want the touch
of my wife's warmth to last forever.

So vulnerable we are, so fragile,
so small and psychologically derailed when we are faced
with the enormity of it all.

I don't want my heart to explode
like a star in an orphaned sky,
I just want a little bit of peace,
a little more understanding of the half remarkable
question placed before me

at the time

of my birth.

BIRDS

It's September, 2002
and while the automobiles keep coughing across
the metallic spines of bridges,
while the blackbird
dusts carbon monoxide from his wings,
an old man feeds ducks at the side of a pond
where in his childhood he once conversed with a turtle
whose voice was not hoarse
or weary.

Across the water
I can see a multitude of children,
brightly frocked, holding hands with mothers
brightly frocked,
heading toward a water park
of hidden joys,
while above in the topmost branches
of a willow tree, a bedraggled raven sputters
incoherently about how it used to be
before there was a garbage can
every 20 or 30 feet.

Female mallards,
their young now pecking at abandoned nests,
float in lassitude,
pay no attention to aggressive geese,
who violently flap their huge grey wings
in response to the continual drone of citification
and while the sun glistens on the water,
a slowly growing brown cloud threatens
next year's green buds that lie dormant
beneath the soil littered with cigarette butts
and condoms.

A tiny sparrow
wrestles a deformed worm from the ground,
while a magpie frowns

in the direction of a parade of jesters
who carry picnic baskets,
            used umbrellas and toilet seats
into the celluloid frames of a soon to be released movie
that depicts the demise of natural beauty
as it sinks into the blackened
western sky.

            And up above,
where the air was once pristine and not infiltrated
by molecules of technological debris,
            where the moon's lungs
were once free of tubercular spots —
a lone eagle flies,
            remembers how the only sound heard
was the inhaling and exhaling of the Earth's breath
before trees fell,
            before concrete fertilized the land
in a grey death,
            before humankind
unleashed its unbalanced scientific mystery
of the elements
            and left the planet
the latest patient of the galactic
cancer ward.

A MUTE BLACKBIRD EMANATING FROM MY MOUTH

Ah . . . be this the broken tongue of a mournful statue
   or have I simply touched the poet's pallet
   with innocent fingers?
I am almost laughable. My eyes, they bleed upon
   the paper, stop the ink flow of my pen, paint
   portraits of demonized saints from a bardo
   only contained upon the canvas of my own
   skull.
They say that Christ walked on water, that Buddha
   gave birth to a golden lotus of insight . . .

SO WHO AM I TO DEMAND
CLEAR THOUGHT?

This torment I endure, it is only the concrete
   evidence of an aging body, forgetful that it is
   only a body.
It is only bones and sinew and a living capsule of blood
   that will eventually be nothing but dry dust,
   blowing out across a sacred river where my voice
   first spoke with the nuances of the moon.

Oh willowy tender heartbeat of existence . . .
I stand naked before you,
   a mute blackbird

   emanating

                  from my mouth.

A DARK MOANING EMANATES FROM THE BOWELS OF THE EARTH

So I sit here in this chair of one million years
    and scribble my own secret nightmare, my own
    cantos of misery, my own apocalyptic horrors
    with a nervous hand.
Be they only deadening words upon blank gray paper,
    miserable, pathetic and without a prayer
    or epiphany bathed in light?
No matter — they must be uttered if I am ever to float
    down a river of deeper meditation.
For I can hear a dark moaning that emanates
    from the bowels of the Earth
And as the leaves wither upon the tree of mystery,
As the womb of the planet tries to replenish itself
    with a balm of fertility,
I witness the continuance of the historical dirge
    of humanity

AND I CANNOT REMAIN SILENT!

Mankind dresses itself in the cloth of glamour,
    negates the shortness of time and lets its heart
    pulsate with subservient beats of vanity.
My aging eyes stare outward, seeking the signs
    that lead one beyond the dull repetitive non-psalm
    that is etched upon the nightmarish veil
    that blinds us.
Oh the world it trembles inside its molecular,
bombastic structure of numbness,
While the moon weeps and the wings of birds
    are broken upon the heavy anvil of a polluted
    skyline.
Oh where be Creation's more benevolent touch?
Where be the psychology necessary to see through
    all the illusionary fibers we have woven
    into the curtain we suffer behind?
Oh I have witnessed the dark bloody hallucination

of the past as a godless, unfeeling cavalcade
of pain.
I have been forced to wear glasses of concrete,
my eyes blinking uncontrollably
As particles of dust fall into my mind and leave it
merely as a vehicle that expresses images coloured
in a miserable burning cloud.
I hear no ringing of delicate bells — instead a horrible
longing echoes in the wind's song,
The desolate surreal landscape is deafened
with a roaring sense of despair . . .
It stands like a blood red teardrop before me
and I quiver.
Monks chant in the back room of my mind,
but their intonations give me no respite
from this agony that I dance with daily.
My long ancient beard is matted with the suffering
of shattered stars and raindrops,
I watch hopelessly as natural phenomena are laid to rest
beneath a blanket of sociological poison.
Oh we unknowingly separate ourselves from the beauty
of life,
Crush its holy mystery beneath uncaring feet.
We plod on, gazing into the blackness
and see not the continuance of the demonic
flaming collective presence that we ourselves
have given birth to.
The serpent has wound itself tightly around
humanity's ankle
And dragged it down into the depths of a moldy
caldron
Where the soul lives in cold misery.
Oh must pain never subside, must we be nothing
but a collection of leper pilgrims,
Limping backwards toward the shadows of past
calamity,
Always enveloped in a cobweb of inescapable
bondage?
Oh we look and we look and we look
but we do not find the inner light that grows
the corn in the field,
That touches the spine of serenity, that allows the snow

its whiteness,
That forgives us over and over again,
even though we spit our colloquial denial
into its face.
Oh the brittle walls, they contain us, hold us
to the skeletal purgatory of this world,
Where insight is abolished by the smothering madness
of demonic moths.
The grim wailing of poets and emancipated sages,
it goes unnoticed,
While forever and ever we allow our ears to be kissed
by the satanic oratory of kings and clerics.
Yes, a dark moaning emanates from the bowels
of the Earth
And as the cold, gray mist rolls in,
We wipe our dew soaked cheeks and turn away
from the sun.
And this moaning, this tragic lament,
with voices added by each and every one of us
at the time of death,
Just grows and grows and grows and grows
because we bow down to the blacksmith
of apocalyptic visions,
Accept them as inevitable and continue
in the slaughter of those who think differently
than we do.
Oh Christian, Islamic, Democratic, Marxist monster
who grips us between teeth of man made ideologies
of non-light and ice and dark magic of debauchery,
May you in time be defeated and put to rest
and may the dark moaning be replaced
by an evanescent hymn whispered
from the inner heart of humanity.

REQUIEM FOR THE BLACK SHEEP

In Vancouver, the circle of creativity collapses inward,
   leaves the colourless dust to blow out
   across the numb streets.
The small bookstore about to close its door,
   swallowed up by a lifeless monster,
   the leviathan chain that wraps its metallic fingers
   around the throats of poets and pulls.
This day in literary history is presented by book malls
   whose bulging eyes reflect back in a dollar sign
   gaze.
They care not for the agony or the ecstacy
   streaming out through the artists' pores,
   but only of the dull, repetitive heartbeat
   of the cash register.
Where in hell is the Canada Council,
   the powers that be, the supposed guardians
   of this country's culture?
Soon the Black Sheep will grow silent on the hillside,
   soon the poets will chant in backrooms
   of linguistic poverty.

Oh city, slowly muted by monetary masturbation . . .
   listen, can't you hear the incantation
   of the muse,

   whispering

   in sadness?

A GHOST OF MY FORMER SELF

In haunting clarity
I remember the absolute abomination that paraded
down desolate streets and called itself justice.
I remember the calculating grammar
of politics, the mashed heads of demonstrators,
the tears of the hopeful.
I remember it like it was yesterday,
when I cursed and wept because assassination
was as common as the blue light of the moon
on a woman's breast.

Was it a time of passage?
A time when the enthusiasm of my youth
became swallowed up by the complacency
of adulthood?
Or did something die inside me,
my eyes blinded by a wounded sun of blood red pain?

Numbed by alcohol and desperation,
I laughed into a face of artificial democracy,

BUT DEEP DOWN I WAS
SCREAMING!

I was screaming because the weird mystery
of the Western World was laced with further aggression.
I was screaming
because logic was aborted by the gluttony of banks.
I was screaming because
symbols of harmony were also screaming,
rushing toward exit signs decorated by neon
and plastic icons.

Ah, downtrodden in spirit,
merely a ghost of my former self, unable to rise up
from the ashes of my formative years, when I believed
that we, the children of previous slaughter,

could make a difference.

What folly, what a tragedy to learn
that the dream of a better future was merely a fairy-tale
construed by the minds of faceless myth-makers.
Even the music died,
replaced by the karmic calamity of disco balls
and polyester —
No more troubadours,
hell bent to echo nuances of truth against the walls
of hypocrisy.
No more poets to bleed
upon the city streets and lecture halls of the damned.

So what am I left with?
A few friends who seldom leave the cave
of their self-imposed solitude.
We meet on worn out carpets,
sip tea, tremble and laugh during discussions
of present day politics —
but there's no fire in the belly,
no galvanizing force with which to experience
a quickening in the heart.
We trudge back and forth
to our workplaces, occasionally make love to our wives,
try to keep desperation at arm's length
with various pharmaceuticals.

The days, months and years pass
while the powers that be continue to impose
their will upon this planet
of spiritual

suicide.

THE POET CASTS ASIDE HIS INKLESS PEN

Ah . . . no angels tonight,
no moon glow caress upon fevered brow
or voice of poetry
to annul this ache I feel
behind the global door.

I long for a sign, a reckoning
that will open my eyes
with foreign sight . . .

Oh give me comfort if my pen should die.

This earthquake of love,
it weeps for sanctity,
but my midnight meditation
bears not a single
candle.

Disparaging face before the mirror,
anguish wheel inside my head,
the upturned hand of Maitreya
resting above a blue lotus
while my internal eye
is smothered
in cataracts of illusion.

Maya maidens alluring,
cause me to relinquish Buddha mind
to desires of the flesh.

Movie moguls laugh in plastic purgatory,
create superficial scenes
where I become a beggar,
blood footed,
staggering over the broken glass
of temptation.

No pyramids of thought here,
no naked and open mouth
with rose petaled metaphors
emanating from my parched lips . . .
just buggery of the soul,
dysfunctional
beneath a blanket of non-purity.

Oh Creator . . . be thou real this night
and release my turgid heart,
rattle my rib cage
with a hollow bone of wisdom,
devour me in thy incandescent
rapture!

I bow my head in silence
and try to remember
the perfect image of a butterfly,

slowly waving its wings

upon an ancient stone.

MILLENNIUM POEM

Is it midnight or is it dawn?
Light flickers like a nearly completed candle,
   shadows dance upon the walls
   of history.
Are they moving in joy or is the subtlety of their
   activity tinted in blue gestures
   of sadness?
Will we move forward, leave behind the confused
   trappings of antiquity?
Will we smile toward a virgin vista, ready to explore
   the possibility, the potential of a more harmonious
   future?
A new millennium, where hopefully the celebration
   of war heros and blood soaked battlegrounds
   will be a thing of the past and we'll pay homage
   to the more sage minded among us.
This precipice that stands before us, ready to receive
   flights of human understanding . . .
Will it be recognized, or will we drop off its edge
   and land upon the frozen, turgid ground below?
This question of paramount importance
   waits in anticipation for an answer

while the children of tomorrow
stare down from a blue sky

and wonder.

EAGLE CREEK

At Eagle Creek 3,000 years ago
a magpie peered out from behind the leaves
of a cottonwood
and saw insects dancing above the water

And she knew that this was good.

At Eagle Creek 2,000 years ago
a deer brought her fawn to the edge of the shoreline,
and they drank and listened to the chant
of a squirrel

And they knew that this was good.

At Eagle Creek 1,500 years ago
a bear stuffed his face with wild berries,
scratched his back against a pine tree,
sniffed at the air

And he knew that this was good.

At Eagle Creek 500 years ago
the first sign of human habitation began
to make its presence felt
as a miner on a horse spit into the wind

And a sparrow wondered if this was good.

At Eagle Creek 100 years ago
a dirt road became a passage to the Rockies
and hordes of mule trains pounded the soil
throwing dust into the eyes
of mountains

And the soil knew that this was not good.

At Eagle Creek 50 years ago
    towns sprang up, complete with saw mills
    and noise and a cacophony of unnatural
    death

And the creek knew that this indeed was not good.

Today at Eagle Creek
    you can hear her flowing by from the highway,
    as thousands of automobiles spew out
    carbon monoxide
    and planes fly overhead
    and garbage piles up on
    her banks.

And she wonders if she can hold on
    and the magpie and the deer
    and the bear and the sparrow
    only visit occasionally,

    while trees stand forlorn,
    coughing and sputtering

    in the wind.

THE LAMENT OF THE OLDEST MAN IN THE WORLD

Oh I am the oldest man in the world and I am weary.
I can no longer feel the sun, no longer does the moon
  enchant me with romantic ideology . . . my eyes
  are now blistered, for I have seen too much.
I have seen Creation's misunderstood finger initiate
  time and space, have seen a man limp in awe
  from the first cave, have seen the karmic wheel
  spin forever with little or no change.
I have seen a choir chant in a cathedral draped in dust,
  while down in the streets, paupers and the disabled
  stagger with empty bellies toward damp, miserable
  hovels.
I have seen a saint forsaken with nails, a centaur
  commit suicide from the highest peak, a poet choke
  on the angst of his own words.
I have seen a naked woman beneath a stone angel,
  seen Quasimodo and Abelard moan from bell
  towers, trapped in the sorrow of loveless beds.
I have seen four horsemen ride away from
  the stable in a dull flash of light, seen monks
  abandon the holy throne.
I have seen armies gathering in Heaven and I have
  seen the eventual outcome.
I have seen the war, the God awful war that never
  ends, that continues to crucify the scared blood
  of Love's forgotten veins.
I have seen a powerful magi wave his blasphemous
  wand and fill our eyes with a dark presence.
I have seen seraphim suck nectar from the hearts
  of flowers.
I have seen the apocalyptic zoo become a reality,
  a rainbow dressed in angry colours, the ache
  of peace banished to a moldy demented
  dungeon.
I have seen a circus of dis-eased raindrops fall upon
  oblivious cities, watched the slumbering cavalcade

of puppets, who, clad in the finery of a timeless
decadence, simply yawn and return to the sleep
of complacency.
I have seen a clown drown in a bucket of his own
tears
I have seen living things not vibrant, only static,
a bastardized wind lust of time, an overflowing
phantom of ritualistic evidence that curses
in the concrete notation of minutes, years and aeons.
I have seen birds melting upon a sidewalk of plastic,
the sex organs of ancient gargoyles frozen,
an artist die in a gutter of rancid
paint.
I have seen frogs born with 25 limbs, trying to move
in deformity through mud puddles of unnatural
light.
I have seen 10 million butterflies explode across
the political capitals of the world, but the leaders
were too busy hallucinating beneath a depleted sun
to notice.
I have seen black lesions grow upon the decrepit
orchard of individualized souls . . .
Oh inconsequential masturbation of non-spiritual
genitalia, the undoing of all that was learned
before we began to worship the industrialized
goddess, who coughing upon her deathbed,
still smiles behind a putrid mask.
I have seen her frozen husband, fornicating between
sheets of rusty metal, producing children
desensitized at the very moment of conception.
I have seen infants wipe tubercular moisture
from their pillows, while foliage weeps
and the planet spins in the direction of a thousand
dark prophecies.
I have seen the thin veil of eternity ignored,
seen the beloved cast out, seen inquisition used
as a symbol for religiosity.
I have seen the front door closed forever, the window
of the mind shattered, the Universe swoon in sorrow
and the dance of the spirit slow down.
I have seen the daffodil weep, the mythological grail
crushed beneath unconcerned feet, the human face

become a mask of indifference and the dove cast
aside by a hand of utter mockery.
I have seen the lament of hollow cheeks disregarded,
seen the ferryman's craft forever empty, seen bags
of sadness placed outside the circumference
of the globe.
I have seen the electronic garden usurp all that was
once green, a robot bless a child with rancid oil,
the moon raped of its virginity.
I have seen the mediocrity of ego-driven philosophers
and the half-baked similes of priests spread words
of propaganda that should only be recognized
by the rotting dust of desecration.
I have seen time march like an unrestrained lemming,
crash into the yawning abyss and fall toward
the future without any sense of purpose.
I have seen laughter avoid an infant's face, poets die
like over-ripe fruit on the vine, turtles rise
to the surface and finding no light, return to
the mud of an endless sleep.
I have seen the perpetuation of grassy fields fed
by human blood, a parade of ghost forms come
back to wander forlorn with outstretched palms,
seeking the sustenance of human warmth.
I have seen the icicle of the world born on a historical
breeze . . . it blows with the heat of a frigid crone,
wrinkled, seeking recognition in the pages
of cataclysmic events.
I have seen our inner power shifting, watched us weep
in undone solitary rooms, spin upon a mandala
completely devoid of nirvanic possibility.
I have seen a distant muse sing from a hut in Babylon
. . . no cadence of clarity, just blues calamity
wrapped up in the hoarse throat
of cigarette paranoia.
I have seen that the archival mantra has been out
of tune for far too long, that we must orchestrate
another deeper level of music whose vibration
caresses the eardrum of be-ing with tonalities
of wisdom.
I have seen children murdering other children
instead of lingering over the faces of embryos

not yet born.
I have seen the haze of technological dichotomy,
blooming hypocrisy on the floor, wooden
and soiled by television evangelists, while illogical
scientists try to negate the beauty
of the Madonna's face.
I have seen the insensitive biological chariot race
toward the ultimate borderline and then stop
short.
I have seen the complacent gnome ruling the dying
land, while the populace, afraid that their
offspring may starve, succumb to his bleary
command.
I have seen the spark of incensed contemplation,
when men could all see through the fog,
but eventually they turned away and re-entered
the mist of a mortal morass.
I have seen the external revelation, seen it simply
to be an illusive lesson taught by guilt riddled
practitioners, fallen citified saints who failed
to see that every individual pilgrim
is bless-ed.
I have seen the bleak horizon, colourless, waiting
for the sunglow light of an unseen divinity
to show its face.
I have seen the metaphysical stone upon which
the slow paced heart is scraped as it moves
forward and upward.
I have seen downtown hobos, iridescent lost angels
who thread their veins with opiate pain relief.
I have seen teenage hookers, street criers with untuned
guitars, harmonicas from hell, moaning out into
the apathetic air.
I have seen an old woman who still weeps upon
her sagging breasts, offering the nutritional value
of her blistered nipples and hardly finding
a thirsty mouth.
I have seen aching broken fingers scratching
upon the human wall while hearts fall to the ground
and wonder why they haven't evolved since
the day the snake first crawled
into the garden.

Oh I am the oldest man in the world and I have seen.
I have seen a leviathan uncontrolled misery envelope
this poor aching planet with seemingly no end
in sight.
But I have also glimpsed the never ending flame,
the cosmic link of light and fire, that which is
beyond our day to day miscellaneous excuse
for breathing . . .

And I have seen that the ancient collective soul
is thirsty . . .

OH SO THIRSTY

FOR

REDEMPTION.

I WANT TO CONVERSE WITH THE SOULS OF TREES

Oh I am weary
of speaking
with the breath of desperation,
so
damned
tired
of pleading
to God knows who
with a crucifix
stapled to my tongue.

I want to stretch out upon a massive rock
bathed in sunlight,
feel the blackbird caress my cheek,
befriend the spirit world,

HAVE VISIONS!

SPEAK IN ECSTACY!

I have no desire to encourage
the demented demons
scratching up the walls
of the city —
No! I want to enter into a pact
with the mysteries
of silence.

I want to explore the adventure inherent
in unseen vistas,
invoke the delicate deliverance
of another dimension,
be held in the arms
of an unworldly benevolence.

I want to converse with the souls

of trees.

Let me come to realize
that the wide open space
beneath the eagle's eye,
the chant of the cricket
and the prayer of the owl
are the holy mystic
brotherhood
of natural phenomena.

Let me crack out of this shell of physical bondage,
shatter this capsule of illusion,
swim with phosphorescent fish
through the waters
of ultimate reality.

Oh single eyed dream of desolation,
Oh turtle back of non-movement . . .

release me from this slowly eroding vehicle,

this slowly eroding planet

and let me fly to the domain

of the servants

of moonlight.

CESSATION POEM

Oh Avalokiteshvara!
Oh Christ's blood that runs down to the base
    of a wooden crucifix!
I will try, I will try to pacify my verbal
    vindictiveness

    and place a rose at the foot
    of the tombstone
    of human misery.

ONE MORE SPIN OF THE WHEEL

A BLESSING OR A CURSE

Ah . . . 52 years without touching the heartbeat
   of the metaphysical garden, 52 years of body ache
   and a soul enveloped in a huge fiery question mark.
All the poetry of the past nothing but a beginning?
Simply a groveling in the linguistic dark, a patchwork
   quilt of contradictory phrases, babbling
   with loose seams?
When young, I crept out into the still, decadent
   night, heard screech owls in the distance,
   felt the damp iron glove of a bastardized muse
   caress my cheek.
I vowed to alter my course, found Buddha, found Beat
   poetics, found the ancient wisdom of Tu Fu
   and Li Po.
I trembled so strongly under Shelley's spell
   that I contemplated suicide at 26, felt a desire
   to be embraced in the perfect diction
   of a celestial language.
Oh, but where be such a language?
Where be the verdant metaphor that will wipe the blood
   from the tongue of the universal poet?
And as I continue in my search, not sure whether
   it is a blessing or a curse,
            I wonder if Rimbaud was correct

when he put down his pen

for the last time.

GOODBYE BLACK ANGEL

Goodbye black angel,
Goodbye to you who cover up our eyes
with the darkness of wasted blood
and a patchwork of illusive gold.

I have been watching
you since you fell from the sky and began to weave
your decadent magic down here
upon the Earth.

You who have brought forth
the blackened rain, ripping the light from our minds,
giving us an excuse to be raped of all hope
or advancement.

You who slowly destroyed
the concept of completion, you who blistered
the child's sight, you who deafened our ears
to the utterance of Eternity's whisper.

Oh love lost,
the once immaculate silence broken down into fragments
of cacophony . . . the misunderstood veil
that you have unleashed, swirling,
crippling us from Calcutta
to Los Angeles.

I watch as all the blind houses
shut off their lights, notice how green fades
into a blackening cold concrete.

All living things gasping
at the edge of a smoking gutter, the corpses of history
enfolded between the pages
of religious texts.

Are we merely meant to be

particles of dust, swept across a limping landscape
where a cruel wind moans from the mouth
of a fiery, uncaring caldron?

            NO! I say goodbye to you
and your imperfect mystery . . . I throw these pieces
of tarnished silver, these coins of betrayal
back into your face

            and allow myself to be bathed
in the ethereal waters

of affirmation.

INCONCLUSIVE LAMENT

And so I climb
from my celestial bed,
place the light of my soul
in an unknown womb
and begin the long road back
to a tender vehicle
of flesh.

Ah . . . but will I remember past animations?
Will I recall if I sat brooding
at the edge of the Ganges,
if I screamed poetics from a rowboat,
caught in a whirlpool
of anxiety?

Did I witness the birth
of great nations,
only to see them collapse under the feet
of rusty politic?

Were they numbed
by man's insensitivity to man,
fooled down below in a catacomb
where death roars
with antiquated lungs?

Ah poor, paltry,
but ever traveling essence
of livingness,
what have you see,
but forgotten?

Oh how many offspring
have tasted breath
as a result of my loins?

How many lovers

passed through my hands,
trembling beside my quaking flesh
in the midnight of mortality?

How many more births,
how many more deaths still to come?

My fate,
my long confused fate,
karmically stretched out with so many lessons
still to be digested
because of past calamity.

When will I recognize
that this never ending tragedy
must be transmuted,
altered by a benediction of kindness,
touched by the relevancy
reflected in bodhisattvic
insight?

Here within the initial moments
of a new millennium,
I look out into the world
and witness a catastrophe
in the making.

I see the mad scramble
of demented ants,
all moving in different directions,
stumbling over themselves,
so many crushed,
so many unable to rise
because the restoration of grace
is an unseen possibility.

The dilemma of the collective purpose,
the yawn of a new dawn,
awakening in the non-light
of a blackened sun . . .
too sick, too weary to restore itself
back to a white womb

of nourishment.

Is this what I have returned to,
a portrait of a broken world,
the frame cracked,
the smiling faces turned upside down
until reflections of sadness
are deemed the norm?

Oh one more spin of the wheel,
one more arduous journey
across this barren
landscape . . .

may the final lesson be learned

this time around.

THE BUDDHA BREATHING INSIDE MY HEAD

I sit here scribbling in the dark,
can hear the moan of Sibelius
as his notes of human longing
float over me
like the juice of an over-ripe
tangerine.

I do not want lethargy
to impede the progress of my soul . . .
rather,
I would cut my body free
from its trappings,
drift away into an unknown cloud
and become rain
for thirsty flowers.

All around me,
birds offer their droppings
as fertilizer for the seeds of the world,
but it is a world
devoid of Creation's compassion.
It fails to recognize the ethereal impregnation
of the soul . . .
instead it turns away,
brandishes metallic sex organs
as a means of protection.

We conjure up visions,
Bosch like in demeanor
and neglect the global breast
that still tries to nurture.

We experience a strange ecstacy
as we approach
the soft warm womb of the heart,
but we hesitate
and then close the trembling pink door

as if it were forbidden territory.

My brothers tell me to find forgiveness,
they tell me that all this ranting and raving
will only drive me toward
a self-imposed
dungeon of misery —

But I pay them no heed
and wander on,

in search of the Buddha
breathing

inside my head.

WORDS FOR A YOUNG POET

The mind moves the hand that moves the pen,
sends it down long hallways of blinking
metaphor.
It does not come to rest,
but rather, rushes toward
yet another explosion of linguistic
foliage.

I tiptoe around the edges of the paper,
carouse with Verlaine,
caress the thighs of Sylvia Plath,
taste the electrified furnace of Dylan . . .
all rising up from the ashes of burnt pages,
all becoming a singular voice,
ruminating in a chorus
of poetic significance.

And the frogs continue to croak
and the warbler still gives song to the grub
and the archangels tune their harps
daily.

Oh this magnificence of sound,
this cat's meow jazz-toned prayer,
it sings into the silent void
and waves back with one million light beams
of vocal possibility.

So you young ones who struggle
with the beauty and internal pain
of the word . . .

Do not let your hand tremble
as you reach for the eyes
of the creative talisman,
do not relinquish
the birthright of your own

vernacular.

Simply be enveloped by your own song
and sing out boldly
into the cosmic quietude.

The mind moves the hand that moves the pen . . .

may your scratchings

be fruitful.

A ONCE CHERISHED BROTHERHOOD

I can hardly
recognize the face I was born with.

Incoherent gestures
are packaged up, placed on a shelf of memory,
where a brand new label is emblazoned
upon the shoulder of my life.

I'm still trying to find
the pathway home, trying to excuse my body,
trying to flee the wasteland
I am a part of.

Oh broken spires line my eyes,
the misinformed gnome creeps into my dreams
at night, carves commercial initials
into the dried out bark of my heart,
leaves me cold at the sight of the instigator
staring at me from the morning
mirror.

Tales of revolution, slogans of peace,
innocent streets locked up in a briefcase
that overwhelmed the hopefulness
of my youth.

Oh children who danced
through the calculation of an imposed fear . . .

let us meet again beneath a bo tree . . .

and touch one another in the incandescent air
of a once cherished

brotherhood.

WHEN THE VORTEX OPENS WIDE

— to Allen Ginsberg,
in memoriam, April 5th, 2001

Oh tender voice,
spinning through a vortex of hellish proportions,
echoing from minuscule pores and the delicate lungs
of unborn babes —
We must hear your often illusive
oratory, heed the mind time configuration pulsating
from behind the door we ignore.
We must listen to the sound of life
in all its simple glory, the mystic chorus
whose vernacular was composed beyond Heaven.

I run like a limping lemming,
entrust my own unholy eye to recognize the seraphim
lining the coffin of history.
I blink 2,000 times,
cry out a whispered psalm in the malnourished words
of a broken voice.
Oh . . . to be greeted from the other side . . .
but this starving song instead wanders down dark
avenues of despair, sometimes too cranky
in demeanor, too often blinded by intrusions
of Maya-mumble, temptress that sucks the life blood
from my aching sentient veins.

Oh arch demon of decadence,
Oh imitator of Artaud and Mayakovsky . . . scribbling
on tablets etched by suicidal fingers, out of control
because society moans from the depths of spiritual
dysfunction.
It weeps down a funnel
of metaphysical anxiety, or blisters the chambers
of the heart in linguistic trepidation.

And this poor swollen planet,

not conducive to rhapsodies resplendent
with a harmonious hum, ethereal essence abandoned,
cast aside, left to wander outside universal forgiveness.
Soft green breasts,
scarred by metallic teeth, gnawed in thoughtlessness,
to fill the coffers of an economic monopoly.
Blue rivers and ponds, once so full of life,
slowly decaying beneath an ozone depleted sun
that tries to rejuvenate itself, tries to reach
with desperate fingers to the umbilical cord
of a galactic fetus.

Oh marriage of earth, water, fire and air . . .
Oh all elements spinning upon the wheel of alchemy —
spin faster, blend all tints and nuances of harmony,
all prayers, all past teardrops into a swirling
circle of unification.
Replenish the globe, replenish our vision
so that we can once and for all see with the clarity
of sparrow and worm and tiny amoeba.
We no longer need blind alliances
that separate tribes, create illusionary borders,
cause the human ego to see differences,
when differences in cosmic reality do not exist.
Mandala, prayer wheel,
wailing wall and vision quest, sameness of universal
spirit . . . only disfigured, marred, in opposition
when we allow cultural discomfort to collide,
explode like a tormented rainbow, shattered into
fragments of colour, in a mish mash of artificial
artillery.

Are we to be half drunk monkeys,
staggering inside citified cages, numbed with anxiety?
No liberation of the heart,
no freedom in the mind, plugged up with the plaque
of pomposity, instead of shakuhachi clear reveries
bless-ed in samadhi.

Oh let us breathe backward
to the essential garden where the seed of existence
was impregnated by the holy eye of consciousness . . .

And I say
Ah to that momentous occurrence,
Ah to the divinity of a mystic finger, tenderly tracing
future footsteps.
Ah to the now unheard music that emanates from
a river kissed stone, from the whisper of a moth's
wing, from the dew dripping from the softest frond.
Ah to all beings who weep in desperation,
Ah to a benediction of kindness.
Ah to universality of the longing human spirit,
Ah to nation states soon to be dissolved.
Ah to my pen, confused and contradictory,
Ah to the Spring that washes the dust from the mirror.
And ah to the Ginsbergian lamb who howled
from American rooftops,
Who opened the vortex wide
and allowed every versifier to sing
from the deepest chambers

of non-biological heart.

*

*

*

*

Oh sweet voiced bard of magic psalm,
gone from this world's empty stage,
gone from the ears of the hungry.
Harmonium silenced, Tibetan cymbals
laid to rest inside purple Buddha cloth,
limping hip and wandering eye now at peace.
Holy Howl, the weeping walls of Naomi's madness,
Plutonium anxiety, starving beggars
and prayers that tried to rectify the aching throat
of the body politic.

Still, gentle . . . still touching my candle-lit sight
  with nuances of tender hymn.
Allen, your wild beard cascades from literary sky,
  all white, but flowing around a softer mouth,
  uttering phrases in prophetic tonality.
You never really left us, the words still bleed
  and laugh from your translucent pages.
Green automobiles sail along Galilee shoreline,
  King of May, singing behind marijuana mind,
  now blessing the children of the children
  you blessed in the 60's.
No bomb squeal in your ear, no planet assaulted
  by the dark monster who haunted you
  from New York City windows.
Just serenity, while bodhisattvas wash clean
  your new body . . .
Another bardo, another audience awaits
  your immortal

vernacular.

YOU WILL WEEP

The whole world weeps . . .
because to weep is a joyous jump start to liberation.

You rest on the laurels of city steps,
wipe the dew from your dawn face
and come to understand that even the planet weeps.

Teardrops of deliverance,
teardrops of sorrow, teardrops spun
from the aching caldron of the heart, falling down,
washing away the mournful cadence of a dirge
created by the subtle validity of existence.

It doesn't matter if you reside in Bombay,
if you wander the homeless streets of Chicago,
or whether you dwell on the banks of a holy river,
you will weep.

You will weep because in your weeping
you will cleanse the dusty garment that encloses
your soul,
leaving it free to smile
beyond the confines

of the body.

OH MOON!

you who have floated in lunar nakedness
since the time of your birth . . .
come soothe me in my reckless rambling,
give me your calm glow
as I scribble down these foolish words
upon the paper.

I am riddled
with the muted tongue
that emanates from my television screen,
I fail to decipher
any hidden value in the newsprint
I hold daily in my trembling
hands.

Where be the promised rapture
of historical soothsayers,
the non suffering unicorn
of imagination?

Oh significant silver globe,
mood changer,
prophetic inspiration of lovers
and poets . . .

give me the perfect silence you blessed me with
on the night my wife and I made love

for the first time.

OF MYSTIC ROSES AND THE SIMPLE ACT OF BREATHING

What mystic rose
   will be placed
   beside my ear
   when I finally relent
   and escape gravity?

Will I hear its florid voice,
   recognize the ethereal energy
   of the sap in its veins?

Oh I grow old, I grow weary —
   body beginning to feel the pull
   of the Earth,
   spirit preparing
   for the biological ache
   to be swept away
   like the dust
   that has gathered
   upon the mirror
   of my mind.

When young,
   one is wrapped in an invisible
   blanket of timelessness,
   happy that the journey
   seems to be long
   and never ending.

And then you awaken
   on a grey November morning,
   recognize your father's ghost
   beginning to emerge
   from your face
   and you realize
   that the simple act of breathing
   will soon abandon you.

Outside the window the mystic rose
  drops its petals
  one by one,
  soon to be replaced
  by the vibrancy
  reflected
  in a ripe green sprout

  stretching itself

  toward

  the sun.

THE DAUGHTERS OF HIPPIE MOTHERS

Young women,
the daughters of hippie mothers,
bring their children
to neighborhood parks.
No flowers in their hair,
no beads or stoned out faces —
just a quiet calm,
dressed in simple tops
and short pants,
frolicking with their offspring
on this warm May
afternoon.

Hey maidens
of the new millennium . . .
Don't make the same mistakes
that we, your parents did.
Sure the ideology was all right.
I mean,
communal peacefulness,
global harmony
and trying to escape the net
of politic
was a good idea —
But we let ourselves get lost
inside a marjauana-ed haze,
let our commitment slip
and found ourselves
in a coffee shop
30 years later,
with nothing to say,
divorced,
lonely,
some of us psychologically sick,
wondering what the hell
happened.

So stay close to your children,
give them your affection

and don't ever gamble
with the illusive
and sometimes misunderstood
concept of

LOVE.

THE SOIL OF KNOWLEDGE

Ah . . .
to behold this vast mystery,
perhaps only one time . . .
to dwell within
this biological chariot
with its wheels
fixed to the ground.

This is the predicament
that causes us
to be mesmerized
by the mythology
that surrounds the possessors
of wings.

Still, there is much to decipher,
down here on this earth.

We are captivated
by the emotive longing
we discover in our lover's eyes,
and by her midnight whispers
when she thinks that nobody
is listening.

We are blessed with the essence
that emanates from the infant's smile,
with the recognition inherent
upon sage like faces,
with works of art
that quietly speak of other worlds,
other dimensions.

Oh we suffer,
we cause each other to suffer,
but we must conquer this affliction
if we are ever to transcend

to a higher ground
of be-ing.

And if it is to be but a singular pilgrimage,
then let us smell
the soil of knowledge

beneath our feet.

EVERYWHERE AND NOWHERE AT THE SAME TIME

Oh I am the eye of the worm,
the yellow breast of the queen bee
and the laughter
of flowers.

I am he who breathes
liquid air over this parched earth,
he who renders starvation
and famine extinct.

Once I roamed the dark caves,
heard teardrops fall onto frozen shale,
cared not if the ant or centipede
were crushed beneath my feet.

I joked with black seraphim,
I relished the growth of callouses upon the fragile skin
of my mind . . .

BUT THEN

I DIED,

passed through the remarkable gate,
conquered my fear,
felt the caress of a lover whose fingers were made
of translucent vapors.

I came to understand
THE PURPOSE OF THE SOUL,
the seasons, the yawn and stretch
of a new beginning.

I no longer have a body,
I no longer feel hunger or the anticipation
of sexual fulfillment . . .

but I am happy

and I am still with you.

I float through your dreams at night,
whisper unheard poetry into your sleeping ears
and try to soothe away
all your pain.

Oh gentle man,
gentle woman and child . . .
don't make the same mistake that I did
when I was a be-ing of flesh and bone,
unconcerned that each individual
has his or her own set of lessons
to learn.

I saw every suffering person
as one to be either pitied or ignored.
Their failures and triumphs
were of no real value to me,
just obstacles cluttering up the vision
I had for myself.

But like I said . . .

I DIED,

I DIED and watched the folly
of my own ego desperately clinging to the corpse
I thought was the essence of me.

But in reality,
there
was
no me . . .

Now,
I am the eye of the worm,
the yellow breast of the queen bee
and the laughter

of the flowers . . .

and I no longer feel the need
to be recognized or honored,

BECAUSE I AM EVERYWHERE
AND NOWHERE AT THE SAME TIME.

I am the freedom of the spirit,
the heart cry of the Universe,
the deep contemplative meditation
of antiquity.

I am a part,
a tiny fragment of light, in the spinning wheel
of existence,

the spinning wheel of existence
that turns forever
upon the axis

of

CREATION.

THE MOONLIGHT SWAN ON THE BLACK LAKE

Oh behold
the moonlight swan
on the black lake,
bear witness to the child
upon its back.

She sails almost invisibly
away from the shoreline,
is greeted
by descending angels
and converses in a language
too old
to be translated.

Behold the lightning rod
of an unseen wisdom,
see how it darts
like a radiant talisman
into the minds
of leper pilgrims,
see how it feeds them,
removes their scars
of self doubt
and strengthens
their once
crippled bodies.

Behold the downtrodden
weary road at your feet,
notice the heavy burden
of those
who went before,
notice how their backs
break beneath the strain
of false enterprise,
notice how their faces
are draped in hunger,

internally starving,
and then notice
how they ignore the perfect fruit
growing on abandoned
trees.

Oh behold the landscape
of your poor neglected soul,
reborn 2,000 times
and still counting,

and then behold the moonlight swan
on the black lake

and look carefully,
because you too

could be the child

on its

back.

LIKE A SEED BLOWN IN THE WIND

The hammering of nails, the agony that lives
on and on, the perpetual, almost numbing ache
that limps like a lame horse back to a stable
of relentless sorrow.
All motion, all movement upon land, sea and sky,
a circle that spins forever and ever,
but without direction — and while children
are born and elders pass on, we stumble,
as if we have never deserted the initial cave.
Still bearing the rudimentary implements of the mind,
still caught in a vortex of confusion
where the wretched hourglass drains its sand
slowly and the biological form of godliness
remains humbled like Christ staggering
up the hill to Golgotha.
Oh the great mystery, it goes unsolved
in a barren land where our plaintive voices
are swallowed up by the tumultuous aggression
of battle drums, political rhetoric
and ism riddled fables.
And as a woman weeps into her hands
and a man has a vision of a thousand mushrooms
exploding from the ground, humanity lies in state,
waiting for the final release

where it will
eventually dance free

like a seed

blown

in the wind.

STAY YOUNG FOR AS LONG AS YOU CAN

A lone piper on a heathered hill,
trees lit by candlelight,
placed there by erudite elves,
while in the ancient mid-summer night
a boat of dreams comes to rest
upon a shoreline of sleeping
children.

Oh darling daughter, my prayer places you
amidst this serenity,
soft moss at your feet,
far away from sorrow's edge,
sheltered, embraced
by the gentle laughter
of fairy wings.

Stay young for as long as you can . . .
because eventually the veil
of adulthood will try
to cover

your eyes.

I WANT TO HOLD YOU UNTIL WE ARE BOTH INVISIBLE

I want to hold you until we are both invisible,
I want to taste the manna of your soul.
I want to embrace your mother and father
  so that I may bear witness to that initial moment
  when the miracle of your conception
  occurred.
I want to feel your pain,
I want to float in your dreams.
I want to caress your womb that wept many years ago,
I want to kiss away all the spiritual scars
  on the altar of your knees and elbows.

I want to hold you until we are both invisible,
I want to swim naked beneath the moon
  inside your eyes.
I want to massage your heart,
I want to drink your tears.
I want to compose a symphony of words
  so that the world may know of your inner beauty,
I want to write a song for your smile.
I want to bless the delicate orchid of your womanhood,
I want to lick the milk from your nipple
  and taste Eternity . . .

I want to hold you until we are both
  invisible.

Let us not weep at the very edges
    of an uncontrolled destiny
because such a destiny was only designed
    for those who long to continue spinning
forever and ever upon a wheel of ultimate
    suffering.

Instead, let us sing an ode to joy,
    let us create virgin psalms that release
the misunderstood essence of the soul
    so that it may break free of the outdated
habitual turmoil that we find ourselves
    staggering in.

I say to you as I say to myself,
    that there is another wheel,
another mandala-ed circumference
    that we may take hold of
and it doesn't involve the incompetent
    psychology
that barters the living breath and blood
    for a handful of dust,
a handful of dust that we will become
    if we are not awakened
from this comatose sleep that is without
    vision . . .

Oh the warriors that gather aggressive
    pamphlets and coffee cups down on Main Street,
they have been transfigured, motivated,
    plasticized and pulverized
by the steady weight of tears and an unnatural
    philosophy
that only sees citadels of separation
    as a means with which to gather
minute and illusionary fragments of happiness.

They have been duped, drawn inside
    a labyrinth of economic mythology
by gods that only weave a spider web
    of apocalyptic possibilities,
wallowing in a quagmire of heavy wallets,
    sexual innuendo and wars,
forgetful that when they board
    the final train
                                        it will be without

                                        a body.

SEEDS

Oh Maya,
you who sit on a metallic lotus,
caressing yourself with a smile
in the dawn light.

Mother of illusion and seductive madness,
unholy harlot,
bastard sister of Avalokiteshvara,
temptress and siren,
whose only form of fertility
is a womb that bears children
in samsara.

I will not enter your blood soaked thighs,
I will not suckle at your breast
and fall into a deceptive sleep
where my mind becomes nothing
but a vacant vacuum.

Instead,
I will abandon your garden
of artificial pleasure
and plant seeds
of Buddha

Mind.

MENTAL ORGASM

Not a chance dear lady,
   no bloody way I'm gonna get stuck inside
   your vicarious vacuum of sexual innuendo,
   I tasted that particular fruit long ago.
Yes, it was gratifying at the time,
   but you know, after a while, the divinity
   of a vagina begins to lose its appeal.

Hey, don't get me wrong, I haven't become
   a monk or anything, it's just that a poem,
   a painting or a song has a stronger pull
   than the biological rapture of copulation.
I'm older now, I want a more balanced perspective
   on life . . .

sometimes a mental orgasm
is more desirable.

THE REMNANTS OF A DREAM

Upon awakening,
I wrestled with thoughts of ambiguous demeanor,
left over remnants of a dream
where I saw bankers and prostitutes
bleeding with stigmata.
I saw an ant hill crumble,
I saw the avalanche of history collapse
from a man made mountain.
I saw how the Earth gave way,
buried every town and hovel,
while immense populations scattered
into the desert of their minds.
I saw furies,
nubile and seductive,
fondling drunken diplomats,
I saw an archangel languishing
in an empty cathedral.
I saw the smoke of a Golgathian fire
encircling the globe,
I saw a child crying beside a dead rose.
I heard the silence of a monk engulfed in flames,
I heard sleepwalkers
stumble inside a labyrinth.
I heard the unblemished pulse of the collective heart,
I heard the mind explode
into one million embers.
I heard the ultimate hymn whispering
from a mountainside
and I heard that it was both
passionate and sorrowful.
I touched the fragile thighs of a fern
and it crumbled in my hand,
I touched my wife's breast
and it wept from the nipple.
I touched the fruit on the tree of knowledge
and found it overripe,
I touched the moon, the sun, the stars

and discovered unseen
possibilities of light.
I touched my daughter's hand
and felt an almost imperceptible tremble,
I touched my own hand
and felt the same.

Ah senses,
why do you beguile me?
Why must the soft mystery of being alive
stay entrapped inside this decaying vehicle
of flesh and bone
and blood?
I want to inherit that other dimension
where I can dance with an illusive dragonfly
through the dark night
and land upon a petal
of understanding.
I want to feel the lips of bygone sages
kiss my withered brow,
I want to taste
the nectar of Heaven.

Oh . . .
I want to see the smile of the Universe,
I want to hear the stillness
of Eternity . . .

I want to know that I am finally

HOME.

RIMBAUD AT HIS DESK

Rimbaud sitting at a tormented desk,
   rain falling like moist birds outside the window.

Young mind seeking to abort the constriction
   of language, his heart racing, leaping
   headlong into a forbidden fire.

Once again I trace my fingers over his pages,
   feel his 19 year old pulse, taste the fruit
   of his wild orchard.

Trees dripping with an almost convulsive imagery,
   a literary lava flow cascading through his veins
   to eventually burn him into submission.

Ah what genius, abandoned at such a young age,
   while today, a century later, students struggle
   to comprehend his savage oratory.

THE FORMLESS FRONTIER

I turn away from this spiritless ghetto
   where the barbarian fondles the dove
   where the crucifix crumbles into dust
   where the dinosaur weeps
   where the child embraces a plastic rose
   where the womb is assaulted
   where the mind and heart become numb
   where the soprano is muted
   where the angel is tarnished
   where death is a myth
   where the war hero is consecrated
   where life is only a T.V. screen
   that blinks back discombobulated images
   that mesmerize the non-searching mind
   and turn it away from the hidden footsteps —
   the hidden footsteps that we must
   slowly navigate
                              toward
                              the formless frontier
                              of the next

                              dimension.

CANTICLE FOR THE INNOCENT

It is night,
the city rests —

I enter a dream
that takes place
on a shoreline,
watch children ride the backs
of seagulls.

Ah temporary bliss,
stay longer than just
this one night —

Let the soothsayers
of monetary poverty
sleep the long sleep . . .

And let me watch the children
a little while longer,

as they laugh,

oblivious to the calamity
below them.

THE LAUGHTER OF A GOLDFINCH

FOR THE LAST TIME

Practice kindness,
kiss a stone,
chase a butterfly at dawn.

Pretend you are a flower,
yawning toward sunlight . . .
and then,
stop pretending.

Be the flower,
accept insects of pollination,
accept your tiny life
for what it is.

And then,
lie down with someone you love,

as if for the last

time.

WHEN I GO INSIDE

When I go outside
I am reminded that buffalo once wandered these lands,
drank water from perfect streams,
ran like a horde of happy children through fields
of dried grass.
When I go outside I think of one billion birds
and of a heaven of feathers beating softly
against a breast of sun tinted clouds
and of the impermanent vehicle
I am at present dwelling in.

But when I go inside,
feel the pulsation
of the collective
non-biological heart,
I become a dream,
a vision,
a possibility of absolute
clarity
where the nomad spirit
seeks sustenance
at the pond of consciousness.

I can feel the presence
of tiny amoebas
swimming within
the veins of my body,
can be blessed by sages,
touch the wings of angels
and interact with poets
and children
who have no pre-conceived notions
of moral right or wrong.

I laugh in a trans theological garden
that only gives birth
to be-ings of benevolence,

irregardless of what history,
doctrine,
or ethical womb
they were conceived in.

I seek words that speak
to an unseen reality,
that reunites me with the broken cord,
that allows me
to reacquaint myself
with the ultimate mysterious
threshold we call death.

Yes, when I go inside
I dwell within
an archetypal dream
and enter a timeless unity,
a vast vacuum of silence,
a reality that is a metaphor
for all that is transcendent
and formless.

CHILDHOOD

An almost silent voice chants messages
    into my sleeping ear, soothes the boy inside me,
    forgetful of the massive ache of adulthood.
I go back to a swollen garden, pick ripe fruit
    in complete nakedness.
Garter snakes wrapped around my wrist,
    scrapes and bruises worn like medals
    of accomplishment upon the body.
Ah . . . sunlight that never burned the flesh,
    everyday an envelope of warmth . . .
Every night the moon was full
    and frog and cricket wrote poetry
    upon the leaves of my eyes.
Tonight, I gaze inward, remember the softness
    of a moth's wing upon my cheek

    and nostalgically smile.

WHERE BE THE SOUND OF DAWN BIRDS?

— Sicamous, July 10th, 2001

The shock of difference
    converges upon me this morning,
miles away from home,
    in this green solitude,
away from the sirens and electronic noise
where one can't hear the sound
of dawn birds.

It's so easy to become entrenched in your day to day,
    back and forth to work,
completing domestic tasks,
    making sure that the household garbage
is taken out,
    sitting with the morning newspaper,
reading the age old samsaric blues.

Up here, we sleep when we need to,
    we eat when we need to,
we bathe our bodies amid a chorus
of chickadee and sparrow
and jay.

The sun rises and falls, the moon blows cool silver
    notes into your ears . . .
nothing new,
but somehow celestial presence
is more dynamic.

Days blend together, you lose track of time,
    idle repose not only a blessing,
but a cupful of serenity that you drink
with parched hands,
    taste for the first time,
slowly flowing down into the throat
of your be-ing,

providing nourishment
and meditative reflection.

Back home, life is so quick and so easily dismantled,
your children grow and leave the nest,
your parents pass over to the other side
and you find yourself sitting
in a beat up old chair,
pondering the immensity of it all . . .

The stillness of the country makes me mindful
of this vast dream . . .

In the city forgetfulness
is the main course

for survival.

I SING FROM BEYOND THE WORLD'S WHISPER

I sing from beyond the world's whisper,
        I pray to an unseen God . . .

We wander together
        beside a half empty well,
watch wounded butterflies
caressed in the breath
of the wind,
        witness the hair of the dandelion
flow out across the green body
of a sleeping
meadow.

Oh life long friend,
        as we walk toward
our ancient days,
        let our pace be at ease,
let our hearts embrace
the children
of the sky.

We have no need
        to grapple with sorrow,
it is only a riddle
for the unloved.

In the still of the night,
        we rest in the wings
of a nightingale,
        forget the ache of aging,
hold each other,
        soul to soul
and dream of April light
reflected in a dewdrop
of non-sexual satiation.

Oh I sing from beyond the world's whisper,

I pray to an unseen God . . .

Your hand in mine,
as we approach the great
mystery

together.

MAY 5TH, 2003 — A DREAMSCAPE

Sometimes one has to get away from the dark,
has to get away from the hopeless landscape
and rediscover that other pasture
that flourishes beyond
the biological.

Meditations on tiny birds,
musings on the familiar and oftentimes forgotten words
of Ryokan, Merton and Rumi . . . old prayers
still relevant in the confused miasma
of mankind's collective mind.

Ah . . . all histories, they rise up and then crash
like insignificant warts upon the breast of the Earth —
all so foolish, all so rigid in demeanor . . .
while the moon floats above us and blesses
the ethereal cycle, the impermanence
of all things.

YES! THERE IS MUCH MORE TO
BE REVEALED!
SO MUCH WE AT PRESENT CANNOT
COMPREHEND!

So I sit here in the May sun and sing
for the sweet peace inherent in the Creator's glance.
I sing for the wasp at my knee, for the silent
tongue of leaves, for the alchemy
of my ever-growing mind
with all its hopes
and fears.

I wash ambiguous thought from my head,
allow myself to be enveloped in the silky garments
of a new dawn.

I dream of past incarnations, of future skies

where the light of understanding glows
with a brighter hue.

I take pride in the tiny gains
made by my monkish heart, knowing that there are
many stones unturned upon the ever-moving
sand.

I bow in the four directions and kiss away
every self inflicted wound I have allowed
to penetrate my soul.

I lie down in a field of Christmas trees
and let the coloured light paint visions
into my eyes.

I drive the miser and the archer
of aggression from my blood, I feel the tender rain
wash the shadows from my feet.

I bathe my lover in sacred wine,
swim naked through her mysterious waters and feel
the space between us dissolve
like a melted chain.

I vow to fill up my hollow emptiness,
I gain strength from the chant of trees.

I taste the full moon,
watch the skeleton of my dulcimer reincarnated
with perfect notes in its mouth.

I follow a butterfly who leads me beyond
the gates of this wanton city, I uncurl the knots
of my internal tree, stretch out its gnarled branches
and welcome a whole universe of birds.

I cast aside the concepts of time and death,
I embrace the hands that delicately pull me
from this dungeon of clay.

Ah . . . all my mornings become young again,

sadness and its coils of anxiety are replaced
by an invisible companion who enters my body
from the top of my head.

The divine comedy becomes eradicated
and I find myself weeping into the eyes of the sparrow
I hold in my hands.

My heart of misunderstanding
is soothed by a newly found dove who flutters
within my ear and whispers a song of patience,
I watch the last star fade away
in the dawn light.

Shades of violet touch the clouds,
2 billion seraphim, with ancient eyes, gaze down
and cure the world of all sorrow.

The serpent slithers away, the garden
rejoices and projects photosynthesized cups
of nectar upon every petalled form
and colour.

I can almost see angels washing
the non-spiritual, decadent dust of history
from tomorrow's window.

OH GENTLE MYSTERY!
OH HOLY MYSTERY!
MAY THE WIZARDS OF FLUIDITY
SEND FORTH A BALM OF UNHEARD
RESTORATION
AND MAY THE PLANET BE BORN ANEW
WITHOUT THE CONCEPTS OF AGGRESSION
OR GLUTTONY!!!

May silence shine in a benediction of green,
may the Golden Flower stand atop its chakra-d stem
and spread its vibrating light
into the darkness.

May the cross of the Earth collapse,

may the sage minded be released from their rusty nails
and embrace those who bear hammers.

May every coffin become empty,
filled instead with wing-ed frogs who chant mantras
of nirvanic intonation.

May ceremonial gestures come together
in a universal embrace of healing, all mankind
under one, benevolent umbrella.

And may I know that this wandering
will eventually take me to the omnipotent nest
where I will become warm and golden
and without shiver.

My body no longer wracked in pain,
my heart unstained, my whole being
unencumbered and free.

RELEASED! RELEASED!

carried upon the spine of Noah's bird, out across
this vast and seemingly never ending
ocean of tears.

My eyes dried, my wounds cauterized
by the touch of an unwritten sutra, all my fears
left behind in a sepulcher of sleepiness,
looked upon as only souvenirs
of my nebulous and drowsy
past.

All despair gone, all cancerous doubt
placed upon the mantle in an urn of memory.

I stare deeply into a pond and see
the ten million Buddhas bathed by satoric fish,
I look into the sky and witness the galaxy
in its constant state of deep
undisturbed meditation.

And as I drift beyond the dark forest
of my soul, I can hear every tree, every frog and cricket,
every owl of wisdom welcome me
with tiny fragments of sound

from the voice
of Divinity.

FOUR LITTLE POEMS TO CARRY IN YOUR POCKET

1

Why do we become so fascinated
when we hold an infant in our arms?

Because it unconsciously reminds us
of the never ending circle,

of the slowly evolving progress
of our souls . . .

Living,
dying,

until we reach a state of grace . . .

Breathing without
the confines
of a human body.

2

Moths, all colours, all sizes,
flutter around a Nirvanic lightbulb
on the cabin porch.

Are we, too, simply moths,
seeking illumination
and burning ourselves up
before we reach our final destination?

3

Again and again
I find myself drifting back
to those renaissance days
when I felt so alive
in a world of poetry,
music and meditation.

Trevor in the tea room of his mind,
chanting from Asian texts,
myself in awe of the reality
of understatement . . . .

A possibility of expression
still not reached
35 years later.

4

Women,
irregardless of their shape, their size
or their psychological persuasion,

are all tiny pores in the body
of the Goddess of Creation.

Remember that gentlemen

and treat them
as if they are

Divinity.

RELINQUISHMENT

Oh green, abundant, yawning song
    of dawn . . .
Oh symphonic tremble of robin
    and crow and chickadee . . .
I long to be enfolded in your dewy arms
    of repose,
free of the trappings, the crippling sidewalks,
    the monotonous roar of tires
    on asphalt
and instead listen to the reverberating echo
    of a distant star,
                                        whispering bright
                                        and unencumbered
                                        in the purple sky

                                        above me.

THE GNOSTIC GHOST OF THE MOON

Three times the moon smiles,
three times the radiant
wrinkle of wisdom
diminishes folly.

The fingers of alchemy reach
toward the collective eardrum
that has been imprisoned
by the resounding echo
of a monotonous lie.

Ah . . . listen to the cascading tremble
of harp strings,
hear the poet,
who rests upon a hill
and caresses
the roots of his soul
with an endless whisper.

Oh what power breathes
from the lungs
of this vast mystical body,
what untold chapters
yet to be revealed?

The unnamed god
releases a stream of fluid thought . . .
cup it in your palms
and drink deeply,
feel how sweetly your lips bloom
at its touch

Oh come to realize
that the tiny flame
you protect in your hand
is but the metaphysical manifestation
of the eternal candle

that was lit before you were born.

Oh wounding wheel called Death,
Oh wounding wheel of blood and tears . . .
I no longer will spin
upon your voiceless circumference.

I say farewell,
adieu to the fear of Heaven and Hell

and embrace instead,
the gnostic ghost

of the moon.

I BRANDISH A FLOWER THAT GROWS FROM THE PALM OF MY HAND

I am a flask of emptiness that needs to be filled
  with visions
So that I may whisper in truth
  at the entrance of the cave inside my head.
Like Zarathustra, Nietzschian in demeanor,
  I walk this mountain with an open eye,
Naked, blessed, calling forth the birds of imagination
  and various forms of ecstacy.
Ah . . . temptations of the flesh, the lure
  of the monetary harlot,
Basking in the metallic sun, shall be erased
  by the profound utterance of a dawn frog,
The eruption of a sparrow's oratory,
  the cadence of an eternal tree
Who sings with an owl enhanced voice.
  There is no need to seek sustenance
At a stagnant pond of non-deliverance —
  Let the nay sayers who manipulate
Their own minds with a numb mouth
  drink from its caldron of blemished water.
I need to rediscover the wider sight
  of the infant's new born eye,
The rhapsody of the ancient sage
  beautifully purified of all contrived
And artificial wisdom.
  This capsule that I dwell in,
This conglomeration of biological necessities,
  it too will one day fall away . . .
Past lovers and friends nothing but a memory,
  old relations only united by the similarity
Of the blood that flows within our veins.
  I will not be captivated
By shadows or archaic sorcerers,
  hell bent to mesmerize and negate
The hymn that sings deeply within the corridors
  of the heart.

No — I will turn away, understand
that this mystery we call life
Can and will be solved if the mind remains focused
like the eye of the eagle.
My prey resides somewhere within me,
honest and without even the slightest hint
Of mankind's wicked intentions . . .
intentions of separation, intentions of debauchery,
Intentions that are bred by a divide
and conquer mentality
That only lead to the historical bloodbath
that has stained the earth since time began.
I cannot be a part of something so cruel
that it even creates an earthquake of anxiety
Within the sacred virginity of the cradle.
Thus I brandish a flower
That grows from the palm of my hand . . .
and step forward,
Alone and unafraid, toward a frontier
yet to be discovered.

SHAKUHACHI FLOWERS

I gaze upon the silent moon,
feel my heart beating
amid a field of stars,
taste the haunt of confusion
that points me inward
to that place
where sanctuary blooms
like a garden
of shakuhachi flowers.

Singular notes
of passive beauty,
the longing sound of a breath,
reaching skyward
in an attempt
to comprehend
the huge stillness

OF IT ALL.

HAN SHAN

Han Shan didn't concern himself
    with other people,
Didn't care what they thought,
    didn't bother himself
    with the inane particulars
    of city life
    or commerce
    or sex.

He just wanted to be left alone.
He was more concerned with preparing
    a cup of tea on a mountain top,
    gathering and chopping wood
    for his morning fire
    or conversing
    with mosquitoes.

No, Han Shan didn't concern himself
    with other people . . .
All he really wanted to do was scratch
    poems of enlightenment
    into the bark of trees . . .

Funny that we're still reading them

    thousands of years
    later.

A DEEP SATORI NIGHT

Stepping out into the star-light,
I chant with frogs,
and allow my wide awake mind to experience
samadhic possibility.
The echo of a cicada
at the edge of a forested pond
blesses me in a rapture of delicate sound.
Salamanders smile
as the surface of the water ripples beneath the caress
of a gentle breeze.
Snails,
slow and engineered for nocturnal meditations,
crawl toward a leafy oasis of fern and plantain,
owls whisper into the sacred quilt
of the countryside.
I drift on all fours
into this damp mysterious womb,
place my face on the dew embraced grass,
notice a spider two inches from my nose,
weaving patterns
where flies are captured to provide manna
for the continuance
of tiny life forms.
I breathe in the dank air,
am reminded of the impermanence of all things,
how birth eventually turns to decay,
how decay creates new life from the fruitfulness
of karmic activity.
Leaves, once green
and abundant with moisture,
fall to the ground, rot upon the hungry soil,
to become spores, mushroom capped banquets
for chipmunk and deer.
I hear a bird's wing flutter above me,
listen intently, can almost decipher
the soft whisper of the moon,
touching every frond,

every bless-ed back of beetle
and centipede . . .
        their bodies glistening inside a union
of dampness and light.

        Oh a silent place, a solitary place . . .
where my heart beats like a hollow drum,
        empty and clear,
inside the nourishing nest

        of a deep satori

        night.

LEAVE IT ALONE

I dust off old poems, laugh at my ineptitude,
    relinquish my pen to the goddess
    of the moon.
Phrases crash into one another, like boats
    without the steady hand of an experienced
    mariner.
Waves of thought incomplete, unable to caress
    the shoreline behind the eyes, unfinished,
    longing to lick the sand of communication.

Ah Marc . . . leave it alone, leave it all alone
    and rest instead between the pages
    of days gone by
                                        when a simple haiku
                                        was enough
                                        to purge the heart

                                        of confusion.

FOR A BRIEF MOMENT I TOUCHED ETERNITY

For a brief moment I touched Eternity,
saw fairies make love beneath toadstools,
heard the perfect prayer of a firefly.
I understood the silent heart of the Earth,
wept in the arms of an ageless mother.
I noticed how darkness gave birth to light,
how the wind was measured
in a sparrow's wing.

Oh crescent moon of effervescent possibility,
Oh onrush of centipede and laughing fern
and spores popping like fertile breasts
out of the soil,
I stare down at my body
and fall to the virginal moss
in gratitude.

PASTORALE

Oh verdant blessing
that greeted native ancestors,
Oh humble cidar canoe
drifting into uncharted waters,
Oh lovely melancholy,
Oh restful dawn!

I embrace you
in my citified arms,
balance myself on the spine of prayer,
give thanks to a motherhood
of non-expectation.

I AM HONEST!
I AM FREE!

I am the harmonious horticulturist
stepping into an orchard
that needs not a single plow.

I am a child without restriction,
brown skinned, my hair bathed in the smoke

of sweet grass.

THE LAUGHTER OF A GOLDFINCH

Images floating,
delicately floating across the back of closed eyes,
caressing me with a smile,
an embrace of almost
surreal symmetry.

I hear a mad chorus of birds,
I ignore city sounds, come to understand
the symphonic patience
of absolute silence.

Thoughts,
images and remembrances brought forth
as I lay here on the grass,
trying to recall by-gone days
when the laughter of a goldfinch was enough
to bring tears to my face.

Such a beautiful sentient be-ing,
feathered in colour, wings gliding against a backdrop
of willow trees.

And snowdrops upon my tongue
and October leaves, orange and brown,
in an explosion of seasonal
transfiguration . . .
the reverence of life giving back to life
in order that the circle
may be completed.

Oh all heartache be gone,
all problematic parables I encounter inside
my unawakened head . . .
leave me at this moment,
this moment when the hum of megatropolis
is of no consequence.

Give me moonlight peace,
give me the mystic vision of the salamander
as it rests upon the surface
of the water.

For I too am fluid,
I too bear the pulsation of mystery inside the skin
and even though I tremble on this side of the karmic veil,
I recall, if only faintly,
that magic moment when two cells united
to give me life.

I hear a multitude of spirit voices
calling from beyond the mountain,
they beckon me forth to an oasis of perfection,
where the whole Universe is reflected in a dewdrop,
where the dis-ease of self-doubt
and ego chain is erased.

For I am he who is not he.
I am not the fingernail biting nervous social slave,
not the tear of sorrowful eye,
not the artificial laugh or the aching response of a soul
entrapped by the confines
of biology.

No . . .
I am simply a single breath trying to find its way back
to the all-encompassing lungs

of its Creator.

ASIAN MINIATURES

1

Smooth face of a child staring into a pond,
  unnaturally still for one
  so young . . .

What does she see?

The face of a potential Buddha
  reflected in the water.

2

I take T'ao Ch'ien from the shelf,
  read his pastoral word
  and forget about
  the mud in
  my mind.

3

An orange maple leaf
  flutters down from above,
  lands on my jean jacket
  like a butterfly
  seeking pollen.

4

Not enough Zen in this notebook,
  not enough tea . . .

How about Ryokan meditating
  in the snow in December,

  a begging bowl

  frozen

  to his

  hands.

OH RISE ABOVE THE TORN BODIES

Oh rise above the torn bodies,
the bodies charred and ravaged with the rape of religion
and politics.

Let your voices echo a gentle laughter,
let them penetrate this night of bloody darkness
where the war pain of aggressive lust
tries to put out the light you protect in the palm
of your hand.

The men of this poor misguided world
sit beneath a decaying tree, while all around them
the forest is burning.

They worship a crooked cross,
they peer through the rubble they have created
and expect monetary redemption
from a neon Christ.

Cathedrals are surrounded
by barbed wire and priests who hold scepters forged
in a furnace of persecution.

OH WE ARE BLIND,
WE ARE SO BLIND!!!

Merely shadows walking
through this quagmire of biological misery,
slowly digging a fiery grave
for the soul.

We stumble naked in unawareness,
cling to one another with spiritually emancipated arms
and wonder why we tremble.

WE ARE BLIND!!!
FROZEN INSIDE!!!

Our lives a useless excuse of mortality,
holding on to a man-made crucifix
instead of staring deeply into the uncorrupted blue eyes
of love's mystic manifestation.

So rise above the torn bodies,
above the closed sepulcher that mankind fails to open,
above the veil that is stitched with a needle of suffering,
above the non-divine bonfire,

and seek

THE ILLUSIVE LANGUAGE
OF UNIVERSAL

HEART.

A POET'S EPITAPH

If I have felt my thoughts too deeply
    then let me be a leper of emotion,
licking my wounds, drying a saddened eye
    in the company of contempt,
ready to withstand the brutal stones
    that be hurled into my heart.

For I am honored to be misunderstood,
    even if it be deemed that I should wear
the crown of the ultimate fool.

Let it be said that I was lustful
    to comprehend Eternity
and that I sought light at the end of my pen.

    If my words be moldy and hackneyed,
then cast them aside like forgotten sheaths
    of papyrus, brittle and unreadable.

And if I have pursued the breath
    of a poet gone mad,
then let me dwell inside the walls
    of those who have ranted before
so that I can sit at their table of skulls
    and feathers
and exchange the horrors
    and ecstasies
of unseen hallucination.

THANK YOU

to the musical poets I listened to regularly during the formation of this book — Tom Rapp and Pearls Before Swine, Oliver Shanti, Nico, Current 93, Sheila Chandra, Bruce Cockburn, George Chaitanya Deuter, Patty Griffin, David Gray, Mark Heard and the music of Cirque Du Soleil

and to the poets of the printed page — Kathleen Raine, Michael McClure, Paul Claudel, Kenneth Patchen, Saint-John Perse, Guillaume Apollinaire, Arthur Rimbaud, P.B. Shelley, Rainer Maria Rilke and Frederico Garcia Lorca.

A special appreciation to David Tibet for his naked honesty and poetic vision.